The Grandchildren of the
INCAS

THE WORLD'S CHILDREN

The Grandchildren of the
INCAS

MATTI A. PITKÄNEN

WITH RITVA LEHTINEN
AND KARI E. NURMI

Carolrhoda Books, Inc./Minneapolis

The publisher wishes to thank Christine A. Hastorf, Assistant Professor of Anthropology at the University of Minnesota, for her assistance in the preparation of this book.

This book is available in two editions:
Library binding by Carolrhoda Books, Inc.
Soft cover by First Avenue Editions
241 First Avenue North
Minneapolis, MN 55401

This edition first published 1991 by Carolrhoda Books, Inc.
First published in Finland in 1984 by Otava Publishing Company Ltd.
under the title INKOJEN LASTENLAPSET.
Original edition copyright © 1984 by Matti A. Pitkänen
Additional text copyright © 1991 by Carolrhoda Books, Inc.

Library of Congress Cataloging-in-Publication Data

Lehtinen, Ritva.
  [Inkojen lastenlapset. English]
  The grandchildren of the Incas / by Ritva Lehtinen and Kari E.
Nurmi ; photographs by Matti A. Pitkänen.
    p.   cm. — (The World's children)
  Translation of: Inkojen lastenlapset.
  Includes index.
  Summary: Describes the civilization of the ancient Incas,
comparing it to the lifestyle of their modern descendants the
Quechua Indians of Peru.
  ISBN 0-87614-397-4 (lib. bdg.)
  ISBN 0-87614-566-7 (pbk.)
    1. Incas—Juvenile literature [1. Incas. 2. Quechua Indians.
3. Indians of South America—Peru.] I. Nurmi, Kari E.
II. Pitkänen, Matti A., ill. III. Title. IV. Series: World's
children (Minneapolis, Minn.)
F3429.L55   1991
980'.01—dc20   90-35507
                                                         CIP
                                                         AC

Manufactured in the United States of America

    3   4   5   6   7   8   9   10   00   99   98   97   96   95   94   93

There is a legend that long ago the sun sent two of his children to earth to start a new civilization. It is said that the brother and sister rose out of the waters of Lake Titicaca, high in the Andes Mountains of South America. They settled in the Cuzco Valley in what would one day be Peru. This was the beginning of a great people that would come to be known as the Incas.

Whether or not you believe this legend, it is probably true that the Inca Empire grew out of a small group of people who lived in the Cuzco Valley. By the 1500s, this civilization numbered over 10 million people, and it included parts of what is now Peru, Bolivia, Colombia, Argentina, Ecuador, and Chile.

The Inca Empire disappeared long ago. But many of the people who now live in and around the Andes Mountains are descendants of the Incas. The people that are most often identified with their Incan ancestors are the Quechua Indians. These are the people we will call "the grandchildren of the Incas."

7

The Inca Empire was ruled by an emperor, who was called the Lord Inca. The Lord Inca made sure that everyone had food, clothing, shelter, and medical care. In exchange, the people were expected to work hard and follow strict laws.

While the common people lived quite simply, the Lord Inca and his nobles lived in luxury. They wore clothes embroidered with gold and silver, and they ate from golden dishes.

The Inca Empire grew rapidly. The Incas conquered surrounding peoples, taking over their land and sometimes adopting their ways. But in the 1530s, the Incas themselves were conquered by the Spanish. Soon there was very little left of the Incan civilization. The Spanish stole its treasures, destroyed its cities, and made its people slaves.

The people we know as the Incas called themselves "the People of the Four Quarters." They used the word *Inca* to describe their leader and his nobles. But the Spanish thought that all of the People of the Four Quarters were called Incas. So in modern times, *Inca* refers to everyone who made up the Inca Empire.

Most modern Quechua Indians live in the mountains of Peru and Bolivia. Tomás and José live in Peru, near the village of Urubamba. For hundreds of years, their ancestors have farmed the mountain soil.

The Incas used advanced farming methods that made it possible for them to grow crops on steep, rocky land and in places where rain seldom fell. They farmed the steep slopes by building giant steps, called terraces, into the mountainside. They used pipes and channels to bring water from rivers and lakes to their fields.

Most of the Quechua still make their living by farming. Like their Incan ancestors, they grow such crops as potatoes, corn, a root vegetable called oca, and a grain called quinoa. Some people still use the terraces built by the Incas long ago.

Carmen, her mother, and her brothers are herding sheep on the ruins of Tambomachay near Cuzco. Carmen is holding the lamb her parents gave her for her sixth birthday. She knows she must take good care of the lamb because her family needs its wool to make into clothes.

Carmen's mother is spinning wool into yarn. When she's done, she'll use the yarn to knit a warm sweater. She hopes to sell the sweater in town to make a little extra money.

Sheep are not the only animals herded by the Quechua. Some people raise llamas or alpacas. Both llamas and alpacas are large, woolly animals that are related to the camel. These exotic creatures are very useful to the Quechua. Their wool can be used to make clothing, and their hides can be made into leather. Llama and alpaca meat can be eaten, and even their manure can be dried and burned as fuel.

Like the Quechua, the Incas who lived in the mountains raised llamas and alpacas. Until the 1500s, the Incas had never seen a cow, horse, sheep, or ox. These animals, along with many others, were brought to South America by the Spanish.

Llamas were very important to the Incas, who considered them to be sacred. Sometimes llamas were sacrificed to the gods in special ceremonies. The Incas worshipped several gods, including Inti—the sun god—and Viracocha—the creator.

Llamas provided the Incas with food, clothing, fuel, and even transportation. They could carry heavy loads and, like camels, were able to go long periods of time without water. This made them ideal pack animals. Cart-pulling bicycles and small trucks have

only recently started to take their place on the steep paths of the Andes Mountains.

Weaving is a skill that has been passed down from the Incas to the modern Quechua Indians. The Indians' work is known for its bright colors and eye-catching patterns. The material is as warm and durable as it is beautiful.

The Quechua wear both modern and traditional clothing—often at the same time. Many of the traditional clothes they wear have changed very little since the time of the Incas.

One popular item of clothing worn by Quechuan men that was also worn by the Incas is the poncho. A poncho is a large piece of heavy material with a slit in the middle to go over the wearer's head. It is very warm and takes the place of a coat.

Like her Incan ancestors, a Quechuan woman might wear a large multicolored shawl instead of a poncho. The shawl is useful for carrying packages and also provides a warm, safe way to carry a baby.

It is rare to see a Quechua Indian, young or old, without a hat. The men and children usually wear knitted caps with warm earflaps. Some of the women wear bowler hats, with turned-up brims, others wear beautifully patterned hats.

Cuzco was not only the Incas' first settlement, it was also their capital city and the home of their leader.

Before Cuzco was taken by the Spanish, it was a lively city of more than 100,000 people. Its palaces and temples were covered with gold and filled with priceless treasures.

Now the treasures are gone and so are many of the Incas' buildings. But here and there, parts of the original city have survived. Some of Cuzco's buildings are built on the foundations of Incan ruins. Walls built by the Incas line the narrow streets of the oldest parts of the city. And most of the people who live in Cuzco are descendants of the Incas.

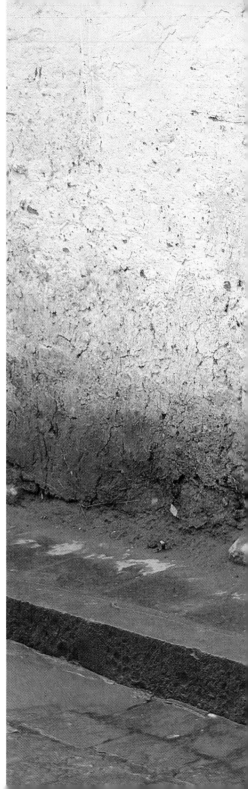

The Incas built their largest structures—their walls, palaces, temples, and fortresses—out of giant stones. The Incan stonemasons fit the stones together so closely that no mortar was needed. The stones held each other in place just like the pieces of a jigsaw puzzle.

The Incas' roads were as well constructed as their buildings. Two major roads crossed the Inca Empire. One cut through the mountains, and the other traveled along the coast. These two roads were connected by smaller roads that ran between them. Altogether, the Incan roads covered about 10,000 miles.

The Incas were such skillful builders that, despite wars and earthquakes, many of their structures are still standing, and some of the roads they built are still in use.

Jaime's mother has made some pies to sell at the market in Cuzco. While Jaime and his father try to sell the pies, Jaime's mother and younger sister do some shopping.

Jaime loves going to the market. There are llamas and chickens and freshly shorn wool. Some people sell sandals and hats, others sell pottery. Fruits and vegetables are piled everywhere. And, of course, there are his mother's delicious pies.

Jaime's mother usually has only a little money to spend, so she is careful to buy only what she needs. Sometimes she barters for the goods she wants. This means she trades something she has for something that is being sold, instead of paying for it with money.

Most of the Quechua have little money and few possessions. A typical Quechuan house is small, with only one or two rooms. Its walls might be made of mud and stone or adobe, which is sun-dried brick. Its roof could be made of grass or tiles or perhaps sheets of metal.

The Quechua eat many foods that were also part of the Incan diet. Some common foods include beans, corn, chili peppers, barley, and many different kinds of potatoes. These foods are usually cooked in a soup, which can be eaten for breakfast or dinner. Occasionally, the soup will contain a little meat, which might be sheep, llama, or even guinea pig.

Life has not been easy for most of the Quechua. Because of the lack of money, clothes wear out and can't be replaced. Nutritious food and clean water are often hard to come by. Even though they are no longer slaves, the Quechua have received almost no help from the governments of their countries.

During the last half of the 20th century, the Quechua have begun to work together to make some changes. They have regained some of the land that was taken from them, and they are starting to demand that the people in government pay attention to their needs.

Many of these changes won't happen without education. Most of the Quechua can't read or write. But this is slowly changing as more schools are built in places where the Quechua live.

Maria and Marta will start school when they are six years old. One of their first tasks will be to learn how to speak Spanish. Their families speak Quechua, the language of the Incas. Although Quechua is now one of the official languages of Peru and Bolivia, it is still necessary to know Spanish to get a good job.

Many of the sorrows and joys of the Quechua Indians are expressed in their music. Sebastian has played the harp all of his life. He was once a well-known musician. Now he is old and blind. He plays his harp in the alleys of Cuzco, hoping that people will give him a coin or two for his efforts.

Pedro's father taught him how to play the *zampoña,* the pan flute. The *zampoña* was one of the instruments played by the Incas, who would often accompany it with drums.

Music and dancing were important parts of Incan religious ceremonies. After the Spanish had conquered the Incas, the Incas were forced to become Christians. Although most modern Quechua Indians are Roman Catholic, bits and pieces of their old religion have survived—especially in their music and their dance.

Lake Titicaca sits high in the Andes Mountains on the border between Peru and Bolivia. It is South America's second largest lake. The clear blue waters are dotted with many islands, including the Island of the Sun, which is said to be the birthplace of the Incas.

Most of the people who live on Lake Titicaca are Aymara Indians. The Aymaras are also descendants of the Incas.

The lakeshore people make boats from dried *tortora,* a reed that grows on the shores of Lake Titicaca. These graceful boats have been used by the lake's fishermen for hundreds of years.

The people of Lake Titicaca are quite poor. Many of them are leaving their villages to try to make better lives for themselves in the city.

Juanita and Teresa live in a small village near Lake Titicaca. The girls have been neighbors all of their lives, but they will soon be separated. Teresa is moving to the city to work as a servant for a wealthy family. It is a good opportunity for her because she will be able to go to school in the evenings. There is no school in her village.

Juanita is happy for Teresa, but she will miss her friend. She would like to go to school too, but she is afraid to leave her family and the life she knows. Juanita will stay home and look after her family's cattle, as she has done since she was very young.

In 1911, a man was climbing the steep, rocky cliffs overlooking Peru's Urubamba River when he came upon a treasure that made every step of his dangerous journey worthwhile. The man was an American explorer named Hiram Bingham and the treasure was Machu Picchu, the lost city of the Incas.

Machu Picchu was probably built in about 1420. During the 1500s, it became a place of refuge from the Spanish. Because the Spanish never found Machu Picchu, it remains much as the Incas left it so many years ago. The jungle has been cut away from Machu Picchu, and the city stands as a reminder of a great people and the battle they lost.

The grandchildren of the Incas have a different battle to fight. They are trying to survive and prosper in the modern world without losing any more of their rich heritage. The fight has not been easy, but perhaps this time they will win.

More about the Incas

How long did the Inca Empire last?
The Incas settled in the Cuzco Valley sometime before the 1200s.
But the Incan settlement didn't really become an empire until the
1430s, when Pachacuti—the Lord Inca at that time—began to conquer
surrounding peoples at a rapid rate. The Inca Empire was only about
one hundred years old when it was conquered by the Spanish in
the 1530s.

What was the capital of the Inca Empire?
Cuzco was the capital of the Inca Empire. The city, which still exists,
was located at the empire's center, in what would one day be southern
Peru.

How big was the Inca Empire?
The Inca Empire was more than two thousand miles long and as
much as five hundred miles wide. It included parts of modern-day
Peru, Bolivia, Colombia, Argentina, Ecuador, and Chile.

What was the population of the Inca Empire at its peak?
At its peak, the Inca Empire had a population of more than 10 million
people.

What language did the Incas speak?
The Inca Empire was made up of many different groups of people,
who spoke many different languages, but its official language was
Quechua.

More about the Modern Quechua Indians

What is the population of the modern Quechua Indians?
The population of the modern Quechua Indians is estimated to be at least 10 million, and possibly as high as 13 million.

Where do the modern Quechua Indians live?
Most modern Quechua Indians live in the mountains of Peru and Bolivia.

What language do the modern Quechua Indians speak?
Like their Incan ancestors, the modern Quechua Indians speak Quechua. Many of the Quechua also speak Spanish.

Pronunciation Guide

Andes AN-deez
Aymara eye-mah-RAH
Cuzco COO-skoh
Inca ING-kah
Inti IN-tee
Machu Picchu MAUTCH-oo PEEK-choo
oca OH-kah
Quechua KETCH-wah
quinoa kih-NOH-ah
Tambomachay tahm-boh-mauhtch-EYE
Titicaca tih-tih-KAH-kah
tortora toor-TOOR-ah
Urubamba uhr-uh-BAHM-bah
Viracocha wih-rah-COH-chah
zampoña sahm-POH-nyah

Index